A DAY
IN
NEW YORK

Photography André Fichte

e·a·r
BOOKS
MINI

ISBN-10: 3-937406-67-0
ISBN-13: 978-3-937406-6-71

Concept, Photo Editorial and Music Selection by Beate Menck
Project Coordination by Helge Trilck /edel
Adapted for earBOOKS mini by Petra Horn
Foreword by Kristina Faust
Translation by Sara Chinbuah

Produced by optimal media production GmbH, Röbel/Germany
Printed and manufactured in Germany

earBOOKS is a division of edel CLASSICS GmbH
For more information about earBOOKS please visit: **www.earbooks.net**

5:35 am - WakeUp Call
Hotel DreamNY.com - 210 West 55th Street

New York is not just a city. It is a myth! From dawn until late at night one can devote oneself to the sexy rhythm of culture, art and lifestyle. The photographs in "A Day in New York" document a day in this exciting city. This ideal trip is accompanied by urban sounds which have been developed by the versatile and ever-evolving music scene in the "City that never sleeps".

The city seduces and intoxicates visitors with it's pulsating energy. Even the tragedy of the Terrorist attacks in 2001 hasn't changed the metropolis' charisma. Since then, business people, brokers and even the police, some of whom were heroes at Ground Zero, have returned to normality and regained their optimism. Many facetted and proud, this self-satisfied melting pot seems to take it for granted that the entire world looks to New York to see what's going on in the fashion studios and nightclubs, and on the streets. An initial visit reveals many familiar attractions, views and street scenes which have been eternalized in uncountable movies.

The city won't wait for you, but it will let you be yourself and this is exactly what real New Yorkers are about. No one complains about the Big Apple, which also has its less pleasant sides, but everybody knows: it depends on you to make things happen; this is why celebrities move about the town so freely. The only thing that matters is what YOU feel like doing! Shopping in Midtown is fun. One can easily spend a fortune in international top-designer's glamorous stores. It is possible to spend sums equivalent in value to a compact car at trendy "In-Places", like the Meatpacking District; with stops in-between for an espresso or lunch at one of the hip bars or restaurants. By comparison, the shops in Soho, where established labels and "up-and-coming" designers present their outfits and accessories, are almost affordable.How about a trip to Harlem to experience a neighborhood coming to it's own?

A lot has changed in the neighborhood; based on the initiative of committed people, who want to offer the next generation a better future. In the middle of it all: Central Park - the city's green oasis. New Yorkers find time to relax in the park and to indulge in their favorite leisure activity: fitness training. No workout exists which isn't being practiced to perfection somewhere in New York.

Regardless of what you experience on your personal journey through this fascinating city, it certainly won't

New York ist nicht einfach eine Stadt. Sie ist ein Mythos Von Sonnenaufgang bis tief in die Nacht kann man sich bedingungslos dem sexy Rhythmus von Kultur, Kunst und Lifestyle hingeben. "A Day in New York" führt mit faszinie ren Bildern einen Tag lang durch diese aufregende Stad - begleitet wird der Trip vom typisch urbanen Sound de vielseitigen und sich ständig neu kreierenden Musik szene in der "City that never sleeps".

Die Stadt verführt immer wieder dazu, sich an ihrem ste tig pulsierenden Kreislauf zu berauschen. Selbst ein har ter Schicksalsschlag wie die Terroranschläge von 200 konnte dem Charisma der Metropole nicht wirklich etwas anhaben. Längst haben die Geschäftsleute, Broker und sogar die Ordnungshüter, unter denen mancher ein Held von Ground Zero ist, zu ihrer Lässigkeit zurückgefunder und sie schauen wieder optimistisch in die Zukunft Facettenreich und stolz genügt der große Schmelztiege scheinbar sich selbst und nimmt es doch für selbstverständ lich, dass die ganze Welt stets danach schaut, was sich in seinen Straßenschluchten, Modeateliers und Clubs tut.

Die Stadt wartet nicht auf dich, aber sie lässt dich ganz du selbst sein. Und genau das macht den echten New Yorker aus. Niemand klagt über den Big Apple, der auch seine harten Seiten hat – jeder weiß: es liegt nur an einem selbst, ob man es schafft. Deshalb können sich Celebrities hier auch so frei bewegen. Das einzig Entscheidende ist, worauf DU Lust hast! Shoppen in Midtown bringt Spaß und schnell ein Vermögen in der mondänsten Stores der internationalen Designerelite zu lassen, ist keine Kunst. Oder man lässt den Gegenwer eines Kleinwagens im trendigsten In-Place, den Meatpacking District. Und zwischendurch ein Espress oder Lunch in einer der angesagten Bars oder Restaurants Dagegen sind die Shops in Soho schon fast erschwing lich, in denen bekannte Labels neben Up-and-coming Designern ihre Outfits und Accessoires anbieten. Ode wie wäre es mit einem Abstecher nach Harlem, wo man auf beeindruckende Weise erleben kann, wie ein Stadtteil versucht, seinen Weg zu finden. Viel hat sich hier getan hauptsächlich auf die Initiativen engagierter Leute, die dem Nachwuchs bessere Chancen bieten möchten. Und mittendrin die große grüne Lunge: der Central Park. Hie finden die New Yorker Entspannung und frönen ihrer lieb sten Freizeitbeschäftigung: der Fitness - kein Workout das hier nicht betrieben wird.

Egal, was man auf seinem ganz persönlichen Weg durch

6:08 am - Pancakes and French Toast
Fluffy's Bakery at 7th Avenue/55th Street

EL Y ELLA - Subway Performer

6:30 am - Subway (N)

6:48 am - Fulton Fish Market

9:13 am - Ellis Island
Immigration Museum

10:08 am - Financial District

10:30 am - Shi Ci Hao
at Sung Tak Temple of New York - 15 Pike Street

CHINESE HAND CRAFT • FENG SHUI

10:45 am - China Town
Canal Street

11:05 am - Mulberry Street Bar - Little Italy

Angelo's Restaurant - 146 Mulberry Street

11:45 am - Relax with your Bags
and have a Coffee to go

Easy Living at the Village

12:33 am - The Field
6th Avenue/West 4th Street

Chess - Games at The Field

12:52 am - Bleecker Street - Greenwich Village

Fashion at Meatpacking District

Florent Morellet

1:04 pm - Meatpacking District
West 14th Street/9th Avenue

Performing Arts - Dancers and Musicians

Washington Square Park

1:22 pm - Flea- and Art-Market

RLING SILVER JEWELRY

l. (212) 447-0041 Fax. (212) 447-0046

ATCH & ELECTRONICS, INC.

SILVER JEWELRY
COSTUME JEWELRY
& GIFT ITEM

ELECTRONIC AND

LEATHER GOODS

WHOLE SALE & DISTRIBUTOR

WATCH & ELECTRONICS. INC

EXPORT · WHOLESALE
ORIENT · BRAND NAME WATCHES

PHONES FOR
AFRICA · EUROPE · CARRIBEAN · ASIA

CELLULAR JUNCTION

UNLOCK DUAL BAND, TRIBAND PHONES
GSM TDMA CDMA

Tel./Fax.
(212)252-9779

525 1212A

AF JEWELRY
COLLECTION INC.

WIDE RANGE OF STERLING
SILVER JEWELRY

COSTUME JEWELRY
& GIFT ITEM

WHOLE SALE & DISTRIBUTOR

TEL:(212)696-2471
532-4601

1212

DREAM NEW YORK

BRAND NAME WATCHES

ELECTRONIC AND

LEATHER GOODS

TEL: (212)683-0335
FAX: (212)683-5314

JEW

Jewelery Stores at 29th Street/Broadway

Relax at the Bryant Park

THE WORLD'S LARGEST STORE

macy's

Macy's - 34th Street

Expert
Shoe Shine

$3.00

3:57 pm - Fifth Avenue

Luxury for Living at abc home

Upper West Side - Swinging Door Men

Cowboys at Martin Luther King Parade

4:05 pm - Central Park
View from the Mandarin Oriental

Mark A. Iocco
NYPD - Midtown North Precinct

Brooklyn - Williamsburg
Broadway Corner at Marcy Avenue

THIS HOUSE SHALL BE CALLED A HOUSE O

5:21 pm Rev. Henry V. Harrison
Baptist House of Prayer - 80 West 126th Street Harlem

6:11 pm - Harlem

7:11 pm Taxi - Ride to Time Square

PROCLAMATION
OF THE
GOVERNOR OF MISSOURI!
REWARDS
FOR THE ARREST OF
Express and Train Robbers.

STATE OF MISSOURI

FRANK JAMES and JESSE W. JAMES

THOS. T. CRITTENDEN

Snapple

Darren Leung
Westside Rifle and Pistol Range - 20 West 20th Street

7:52 pm Robert D'Amodio - NYPD Mounted Unit

The Longest Yard - Promotion Show at TRL

8:15 pm - Times Square

Star Wars - Episode III - Revenge of the Sith - Premiere

9:00 pm - Dinner at Serafina's
210 West 55th Street

VANA and Ute Lemper

Carolyn & Sam Williams

AVA Lounge Balcony
210 West 55th Street

THE BLUE NOTE 131 West 3rd Street

4:22 am - Taxi to the Dream Hotel

Don't worry Taxi Driver
is just a movie.

Hotel DreamNY.com - 210 West 55th Street

A Day In New York
28 x 28 cm
103 photos, 120 pgs.
4 Music CDs
ISBN-10: 3-937406-42-5
ISBN-13: 978-3-937406-42-8

Gefällt Ihnen dieses Buch?
Noch mehr Bilder und Musik genießen Sie
im earBOOKS Großformat.

If you liked this book,
you will enjoy the large format earBOOKS
with additional music and pictures.

CD

1 Lionel Hampton: On The Sunny Side Of The Street 5:10
(McHugh, Fields / arr. Quincy Jones) BMI, ASCAP
℗ 1999 Twinz Records
taken from the album "90th birthday Celebration" with courtesy of Twinz Records

2 Zoom: Jacques Cousteau 5:00
(J.B. Bocle) Choroni Music (ASCAP, SACEM)
℗ 2005 Twinz Records
taken from the album "Love Junket" with courtesy of Twinz Records

3 Vana: Gatinha Sabidinha (Wise Little Cat) 7:12
(Werner Gierig) Vana Gierig Music (SESAC)
℗ 2003 Twinz Records
taken from the album "A new Day" with courtesy of Twinz Records

4 Vana: A New Day 5:03
(Werner Gierig) Vana Gierig Music (SESAC)
℗ 2003 Twinz Records
taken from the album "A new Day" with courtesy of Twinz Records

5 Lionel Hampton: Exactly Like You 3:22
(McHugh, Fields / arr.: Lionel Hampton) EMI
℗ 1999 Twinz Records
taken from the album "90th birthday Celebration" with courtesy of Twinz Records

6 Cedar Walton Trio feat. Dale Barlow: My Heart Stood Still 8:44
(Rodgers & Hart) Warner Bros.
℗ 1999 Twinz Records
taken from the album "Manhattan Afterhours" with courtesy of Twinz Records

7 Vana: Low Features 6:25
(Werner Gierig) Vana Gierig Music (SESAC)
℗ 2003 Twinz Records
taken from the album "A new Day" with courtesy of Twinz Records

8 Acappella Soul: Morse Code 2:14
(Trad.)
℗ 2005 Acapella Soul
with courtesy of Acapella Soul

9 Duo Live: Tough Guys 1:32
(duo live)
℗ 2005 redemption Music Group Inc.
taken from the album "Free Lunch" with courtesy of redemption Music

10 Duo Live: Let's Get Blown Freestyle 1:21
(duo live)
℗ 2005 redemption Music Group Inc.
taken from the album "Free Lunch" with courtesy of redemption Music

11 Zoom: Moishe, Moishe
(J.B. Bocle) Choroni Music (ASCAP, SACEM)
℗ 2005 Twinz Records
taken from the album "Love Junket" with courtesy of Twinz Records

12 Cedar Walton Trio feat. Dale Barlow: I Want To Be Happy 6:37
(Vincent Youmans, Irving Caesar) Warner Chappell Music
℗ 1999 Twinz Records
taken from the album "Manhattan Afterhours" with courtesy of Twinz Records

This compilation ℗ 2005 edel CLASSICS GmbH

**We would like to thank the following people
for their unbreakable support:**

Jennifer Lenihan/New York City Major's Office of Film, Theatre and Broadcasting;
Aida Brandes; Lamont Hampton/Sumont Prod.; Manfred Knoop, Heike Bachmann/TWINZ Rec.;
Brendan McNamara/Dream Hotel; Lt. Mark A. Iocco/NYPD; Frank Paterno; Patricio Osses;
Rev. Darren Ferguson and Curtis Blow, HipHop Church; Rev. Henry V. Harrison;
The Blue Note; The Groove; The Café Wha?.